Dear Parent:
Your child's love of reading starts here!

Every child learns to read in a different way and at his or her own speed. You can help your young reader improve and become more confident by encouraging his or her own interests and abilities. You can also guide your child's spiritual development by reading stories with biblical values and Bible stories, like I Can Read! books published by Zonderkidz. From books your child reads with you to the first books he or she reads alone, there are I Can Read! books for every stage of reading:

SHARED READING
Basic language, word repetition, and whimsical illustrations, ideal for sharing with your emergent reader.

BEGINNING READING
Short sentences, familiar words, and simple concepts for children eager to read on their own.

READING WITH HELP
Engaging stories, longer sentences, and language play for developing readers.

READING ALONE
Complex plots, challenging vocabulary, and high-interest topics for the independent reader.

ADVANCED READING
Short paragraphs, chapters, and exciting themes for the perfect bridge to chapter books.

I Can Read! books have introduced children to the joy of reading since 1957. Featuring award-winning authors and illustrators and a fabulous cast of beloved characters, I Can Read! books set the standard for beginning readers.

A lifetime of discovery begins with the magical words "I Can Read!"

Visit www.icanread.com for information on enriching your child's reading experience.
Visit www.zonderkidz.com for more Zonderkidz I Can Read! titles.

If you stay away from sin you will be
like one of these dishes made of purest gold—
the very best in the house—so that Christ himself
can use you for his highest purposes."
—2 Timothy 2:21

Mrs. Rosey Posey and the Fine China Plate
Text copyright © 2008 by Robin's Ink, LLC
Illustrations copyright © 2008 by Christina Schofield

Requests for information should be addressed to:
Zonderkidz, *Grand Rapids, Michigan* 49530

Library of Congress Cataloging-in-Publication Data

Gunn, Robin Jones, 1955-
  [Mrs. Rosey-Posey and the chocolate cherry treat]
  Mrs. Rosey Posey and the fine china plate / story by Robin Jones Gunn ; pictures by
Christina Schofield.
      p. cm. -- (I can read! Level 2)
  Summary: Natalie learns a lesson about making choices from Mrs. Rosey-Posey who
also introduces a Bible verse from the second book of Timothy.
  ISBN: 978-0-310-71578-8 (softcover)
  [1. Choice--Fiction. 2. Conduct of life--Fiction. 3. Christian life--Fiction.] I. Schofield,
Christina (Christina Diane), 1972- ill. II. Title.
  PZ7.G972Mqf 2008
  [E]--dc22

                                                                2007034320

Published in association with the Books & Such Literary Agency, 52 Mission Circle,
Suite 122, PMB 170, Santa Rosa, California 95409-5370, www.bookandsuch.biz

Zonderkidz is a trademark of Zondervan.

Editor: Betsy Flikkema
Art direction: Jody Langley
Cover design: Sarah Molegraaf

Printed in China

10 11 12 /SCC/ 5 4 3 2

I Can Read!

Mrs. Rosey Posey
and the Fine
China Plate

story by Robin Jones Gunn

pictures by Christina Schofield

Right in the middle of Poppyville

at the end of Merry Lane

stands a big yellow house.

Mrs. Rosey Posey lives here.

Children love Mrs. Rosey Posey.

Poppyville

One sunny day, Natalie came over.

She sat on the steps and didn't play.

Mrs. Rosey Posey said,

"Mercy me, what is the matter?"

"It's not fair," said Natalie.

"All my friends went to a movie."

"Why didn't you go?"

asked Mrs. Rosey Posey.

"My mom and dad said I couldn't go.
They said it's not the kind of movie
I should see," said Natalie.

"Mercy me! You're right,"

said Mrs. Rosey Posey.

"That isn't fair to your friends."

"Not fair to them?" said Natalie.

"What about me?"

Mrs. Rosey Posey smiled.

"Natalie, you have been set apart."

"Set apart?" asked Natalie.

"What does that mean?"

"Come with me and I'll show you,"
said Mrs. Rosey Posey.

They went into the kitchen.

Mrs. Rosey Posey took out a bowl

of cherries dipped in chocolate.

"YUM!" Natalie said.

"Would you like some?"

Mrs. Rosey Posey asked.

"Oh yes, please," said Natalie.

Mrs. Rosey Posey went to the trash.

She found a dirty paper plate.

"Would you like your cherries

on this plate?" she asked.

"Is that the only plate you have?"

asked Natalie.

"Oh no! I have other plates.

Clean plates. Special plates.

Plates that I have set apart,"

said Mrs. Rosey Posey.

Mrs. Rosey Posey held up

a fine china plate with blue trim.

"This plate is beautiful,"

said Natalie.

"Yes, it is," said Mrs. Rosey Posey.

"Which plate would you like to use?"

Natalie chose the fine china plate.

Mrs. Rosey Posey said,

"I have kept this plate set apart.

Now it is clean and ready."

Mrs. Rosey Posey put
chocolate cherries on it.
Then she served Natalie.

"You are like this china plate,"
said Mrs. Rosey Posey.
"You are set apart.

Your parents are helping you
make good choices.
These choices keep you
clean inside."

"Is that why they said

I couldn't go to the movie?"

asked Natalie.

"Indeed!" said Mrs. Rosey Posey.

"Your parents love you

very much. And so do I."

Mrs. Rosey Posey smiled.

Her eyes had a twinkle.

Her smile had a zing.

Mrs. Rosey Posey had a secret.

"Natalie, what kind of plate

would you like to be?"

"I would like to be

a fine china plate," said Natalie.

Mrs. Rosey Posey wrote

on the back of the fine china plate.

She gave the plate to Natalie.

"Is this for me? Thank you.

What does this Bible verse say?"

asked Natalie.

"It says if you stay away from sin,

you will be like a plate

made of pure gold.

Then Jesus can use you

for his important work."

"Wow!" Natalie said.

"You mean the secret

of the china plate is in the Bible?"

"Of course!" Mrs. Rosey Posey said.

"That's where I get all my secrets."

Natalie hugged Mrs. Rosey Posey.

"You make me feel so special."

"You are special, Natalie.

You have been set apart

just like a fine china plate."